PICTURES in the MIND

Glen L. Blesi

Copyright © 2025 Glen Blesi
All cover art copyright © 2025 Glen Blesi
All Rights Reserved

No part of this book may be reproduced or transmitted in any form or by any means, electronic or mechanical, including photocopying, recording, or by any information storage and retrieval system, without permission in writing from the author.

Publishing Coordinator – Sharon Kizziah-Holmes

Indie Pub Press
Springfield, Missouri

ISBN -13: 978-1-964559-71-1

Acknowledgements

A small number of people have especially given me encouragement in my poetry writing or writing in general. These include sisters Bonnie Stephens, Janet Carr and Joycelyn Wainwright; niece, Joellen Wood; cousin Brad James and friends Mark A. Williams and David S. Powell. Thank you for your encouragement. I became involved with the Springfield, Missouri, branch of Missouri State Poetry Society once again after an absence of more than 20 years. My poet friends kept bringing their books of poetry to the meetings to read from. For a couple of years, I resisted the idea of having my own book of poetry. But the more I saw others with their books, the more I was attracted to the idea.

A special thanks also to my son, Zachary, for helping me with the illustrations. I think he enjoyed it, maybe, a little.

Introduction

I like to think that my poems are more honest, more revealing of myself, than those in many books of inspirational poetry that I see. I find many of them a little dry, redundant, with not enough variety. The content is true enough, but it could be said using more precise, self-condemning, or even self-affirming, language. It is said that much of today's worship songs are more about the songwriters than about praise to God. These aren't songs, but I include both—lines about God and lines about myself and others. Disclaimer: Some readers may not agree with certain things I say. Oh, well. God didn't make us to all think the same. We are greater and more interesting than robots. A few of the poems won't necessarily have inspirational value. But they're revealing of me, of what I think about and of what I struggle with.

THIS is the third title I have considered for the collection. The first was too academic. The second was better and I thought I would go with it. It was taken from the very first poem I remember writing, below. Then I suddenly recalled a sort of vision I had way back, probably before I ever wrote anything besides classwork and letters. I had in mind a title for a book I believed I would one day write. When I thought of that, I knew I had to use it. Incredibly, at this writing an internet search reveals no other book with this exact title.

IN the fifth grade, I wrote my first poem of memory. It happened after I'd read some poetry in a book or magazine by some of my agemates at the time. Mrs. Evelyn Simpson was my teacher, probably my favorite throughout school. She provided a fabulous classroom library that I would peruse regularly. I obviously didn't care much for the poems I saw in that publication. Here's my poem.

    Poems have different feelings
    Poems have different ways
    Some don't know with whom they're dealing
    Some aren't just a bunch of plays
    O, I'm not saying mine are good
    I'm not saying they're bad
    I'm just saying that if I could
    I would make you feel more glad

DURING THE NIGHT

DREAMS ESCAPING

My dreams try to escape

And come into the flesh and blood.

I reach for a pair of shoes

Just on the verge of waking,

Or step into a room

And have it turn into my conscious self.

Maybe they feel trapped,

As I sometimes do,

And desire a different reality.

Sometimes there are people

I wish I could bring with me,

Across the threshold,

People I can't forget,

And prefer were a greater part of my life,

As they once were.

Dreams that Won't Let Us Forget

How vivid and factual are some faces in our dreams—

Faces of those who in the past had a mighty part in our lives!

The dreams help to keep their images clear and not readily forgotten,

Help to keep their role in our lives strong and foremost in our minds.

These dreams remind us that those near ones will again

Be part of our lives in God's great Kingdom we long to see.

NIGHTTIME PRIORITIES

The desire for fellowship and communion
With God in the night
Is a compulsion often more powerful
Than rest or sleep.
I can't help but think of the things
He's brought me through,
Of late and lifelong.
I marvel at how He's kept me going,
And given me unending resilience,
At how He's kept me aware
Of my dual citizenship.
I'm in the world but not of it.
My true home is still ahead.
With that in mind,
The trials of this life
Should never get me down.

Reality in Dreaming

Each morning when I wake
May my thoughts, first thing,
Turn to You
If they're not already there
From my dream.
May my dreams be of You
And of Your kingdom to come,
Their intensity sustain me all the day.
May I know the physical world
Is not the ultimate reality,
But only the new world
You're preparing is,
Slowly being revealed to us
As we're here on earth.

THE AWAKENING STORM

A storm in the night lends itself to humbling fellowship with God,
An audible and visual assurance that He's near.
It soothes the disappointments, the indifference of the day—
God's invitation to sense His presence and His power,
Even if my mood seems to hinder the sense of His closeness,
A storm can become to me
God's initiation into splendid conversation with Him.

My Dream Director

I wish I were as good a writer
As my dream director.
He captures people in my life
In all their glory,
Or in all their folly.
He's great at caricature,
And hyperbole,
And even understatement.
But then he'll show me someone I recognize
But just can't place,
Leaving me ponderin' on it for days.
He creates spectacular settings
That I'd never think of,
Rugged hillsides requiring
Maneuvers amongst boulders,
Quaint country cottages
Where dwell quaint
Country people.
He shows houses in my past
In their exact detail,

Never staying in just one room.

He shows me the church, and its grounds,

A significant part of my early life,

Just as I remember.

He surprises with sounds

Stunning in their loudness.

He can even make me ashamed,

Or angry,

When he paints me with colors

That leave me wondering

If that could be

My true character.

The Hazards of Sleep

O that I didn't have to sleep.
I'd choose a starting point—
A time of perfect
Communion with the Lord.
I'd stay awake so that the closeness
Would not end.
His faithfulness is new every morning,
But mine lacks consistency.
By dawn my mind is filled
With countless concerns,
As I struggle to renew
Our communion each day.

LOOKING TO ETERNITY

GENEALOGY IN HEAVEN

In the kingdom of heaven we likely won't
Trace physical lineage—
Too many gaps in the chart.
But our spiritual line
Will be ever so precious
And all involved
Will be there to interview—
No more regrets we didn't ask
While he or she was living on earth.
We'll learn who influenced who for Christ
Until it passed down to us.
Not a straight line
But a tree
With multiple branches—
A genealogist's delight.

Glimpsing Heaven

"Eye hath not seen. . .neither have entered
into the heart of man, the things
God hath prepared for them that love him. . .",
Paul quotes from an unknown source.
But read on.
Those who have the Spirit
and mind of Christ
are able to know
the things God freely gives us.
Not a full knowledge,
but a glimpse,
and that is enough
to keep our hope alive.
My mind races with a perception
of how Heaven might be—
what the music might sound like,
music that I'll no doubt
have a part in performing;
which friends and family members
from all ages might be there;

the likelihood that I'll meet all those
whose salvation I've had a part in;
what undeveloped dreams I've had on Earth
That I may be allowed to pursue there;
who my neighbors might be;
multiple skills we'll be able to acquire
through the ages;
participation, with the angels,
in singing praises to our King,
the most beautiful music we'll ever hear,
perhaps getting better and better through the ages.

Nothing Here Compares

Many locales on earth I've not yet seen.
But none of them will compare
to the sites I'll see in heaven.
I've never swum the Colorado.
But it's nothing like the waves I'll ride in heaven.
Countless books I've not yet read.
But there I'll read God directly.
Many lines I still want to write.
But I'll have time for that and more in heaven.
I've heard countless concerts in this earthly realm.
But together they won't compare with the first time
I hear an angelic choir.
There's so much I still want to learn.
But the training there will the more delight my senses.
So many people I've longed to meet,
and I'll get to know them all when that day comes.
But mostly I'll more fully know the greatest Friend
anyone could ever have.

IN THE FULLNESS OF TIME

When the times comes

It will be the most natural thing—

How we perceive God when in Heaven.

But for now we're curious.

How can we be close to a Spirit,

Whom we may not be able to see directly?

Certainly we'll sense Him,

And we'll see His Son.

What about the Holy Spirit?

How will we perceive the Third?

By any measure it's a mystery

That those who know God yearn

To have revealed in the

Fullness of time.

New and Improved Earth

Certainly new,

But improved is understated.

I think of the prospect more and more each day.

No sin, no threat, no danger!

Utopia in the true sense!

Paradise unrivaled!

Yet with similarities to what we know now—

Canyons we can roll down into without harm—

Bodies of water that require no life jackets—

More than enough to explore—

Harmony among all residents—

Praising God with the angels!

The Angels in Heaven

How will we interact with angels in Heaven?
Will we thank them for their loyalty to the King of Heaven?
Will we have any as close friends?
Or will they be ever taking to flight,
Moving on to another area to praise our God?
What will be their role there?
Who will they offer aid to?
Will their role change as
Eternity rolls along?
Will we simply ever enjoy their
Magnificent singing as they praise the King?

PERSECUTION

LIVING AS A CHRISTIAN IN A RADICAL MUSLIM NATION

What would it be like living as a Christian
In a radical Muslim nation?
When your husband or father is killed for being a Christian,
To suffer depression for months afterward?
To feel anger toward God that you can't control?
To struggle to earn your living,
But to eventually forgive and carry on
The Kingdom work of the martyred one?

Living as a Christian in China

What would it be like to be part of an independent church,
Not registered or authorized by the government,
For the pastor to be regularly interrogated
And the landlords pressured into evicting churches?
To be forced to break up into house churches
To escape harassment from the authorities?
To be forced to move to South Korea,
Where fear of China forces the government
To not allow asylum?
Thank You, Lord, that we still have freedom
To worship comfortably.
Thank You that the church in China
Continues to grow in spite of the persecution.

103. "FUENTE" OBSEQUIO DE LA COLONIA CHINA.—LIMA.

LIVING AS A CHRISTIAN IN INDIA

What would it be like
to have the radical arm
of a dominant false religion
cut off simple benefits
you're entitled to?
To be beaten so badly
that you have permanent damage?
To live in a democracy that
officially guarantees freedom of religion
but unofficially works toward freedom
from all religions but that of its choice?
To have a prime minister who looks
the other way when churches and Christians
are attacked and sometimes murdered?
To have to pretend to be a Hindu
to hold a better-providing job,
but live as a Christian away from work?
Lord, hold not this duplicity against them.
For I know not what I would do
if I lived in this land.

LIVING AS A CHRISTIAN IN NIGERIA

What would it be like
To have a radical at-large militant group
Without centralized headquarters,
Regularly target Christian communities
In your area, killing thousands each year?
To have the crops you need for survival
Destroyed by the terrorists,
Your land confiscated,
Your home burned?
To not have the money to send
Your children to school,
And if they are in school,
To live with the threat
Of having them kidnapped,
So that you're forced to pay a ransom
For their return to you?
Lord, empower the faith of Your people
Experiencing this kind of persecution.
Soften the hearts of their enemies.
And may we not forget to urgently
And regularly pray for them.

Fulani Men, Northern Nigeria

Regimental Sergeant Major, Nigeria Regiment, W.A.F.F.

LIVING AS A CHRISTIAN IN NORTH KOREA

What would it be like to live as a Christian in North Korea,
where radios are banned so that you can't hear
about the outside world,
where Christmas gifts have to be given in secret,
where people are told that Christianity
is a tool of the upper class,
used to oppress those beneath them,
where children are taught early through textbooks,
movies, TV shows and novels
how bad Christianity is,
but where so much evil makes multitudes
of people open to the message of the Gospel?

NORTH KOREA

Un concert, en Corée   A concert, Corea

Living as a Christian in Rural Mexico

What is it like living as a Christian in Rural Mexico?
To be beaten with rifle stocks,
To have a gun put to your head,
The trigger pulled, but being spared
Because God jammed it,
Having your clothes soaked with gasoline,
But spared again when God prevented
The matches from striking,
Having your phones and truck stolen,
Being threatened with death if you tell
What has been done to you,
But to have even more determination
To spread the gospel after persecution.

Tortillera Mexicana.

Camino de México a Acapulco. La Cañada del Zopilote.

Living as a Christian in the Central African Republic

What would it be like to live as a Christian in the Central African Republic,

A nation which outsiders consider a predominately Christian nation,

Where the nominal Christians can only be called non-Muslims,

And help in the persecution of Biblical Christians?

Where half of the displaced persons live in camps.

While away from their homes, Muslims come in

And claim their homes, preventing the Christians from returning.

Where often they have fled their homes after seeing

Their men and boys killed,

And in the camps they have little to eat,

A new militant Islamic group destroying churches

And the houses of their members,

Often killing the people.

May we not neglect to pray for them

And pray we not have to face what they're facing.

LIVING AS A CHRISTIAN IN UZBEKISTAN

What would it be like to live as a Christian in Uzbekistan?

To have your children kidnapped from your place of employment

And then beat you for your faith,

Or have you placed in a psychiatric hospital,

Where you're given shots that prevent you from

Walking, or even thinking straight?

Shots that are followed up by medicine

To make you weak and incapacitated?

To need a few years to recover from the ordeal?

г. Самаркандъ. Главная ул. въ Старомъ городѣ.

Living as a Christian Leader in Cuba

What would it be like living as a Christian leader in Cuba,
And receive death threats, telephone harassments,
To be often summoned to appear before the government,
For your family to be denied education and employment rights,
To have your worship services interrupted by police,
To have possessions and livelihood taken from you,
Yet to retain your joy and vibrancy and your commitment
To God and to His Lamb,
To with the angels in the last day be able to give Him
Blessing and glory and wisdom and thanksgiving
And honor and power and might?

Living in a Jumbled World

Our schools and institutions are denying
What is past.
They're allowing things that alter our perception
In the world and 'mongst our young, to our dismay.
Our longtime cherished heroes have been tainted now by lies.
Beginning with explorers they've misunderstood the times
And told lies about the motives of one Cristóbal Colón.
The memory of Jefferson they've maligned down by the river,
And removed his very name from very land he added.
They seek to wipe away such aspects of our history
As don't suit the tales they wish to teach our children.
Aid is being given to the foes of our own allies
And assistance to those allies highly questioned.
We're told that we're all racists
Due to pigments of our skin tone,
That there's nothing left to do but to admit it.
Yet the very ones condemning us
Are the bigots most of all.
Those who've lived here for some time
Hardly recognize our land.
Our values are not what they used to be.

We question where we're headed and wish we could go back
To the days when we were innocent and carefree.

WHAT THE PERSECUTED CHURCH ASKS OF US

Pray—

That we remain faithful when pressured

Pray—

That we not deny our Lord to get leniency

Pray—

That we do not hate our oppressors

Pray—

That survivors earn their living without compromise

Pray—

For our assurance the Christian world cares

Personal Reflections

ADDICTED TO LIFE

Sometimes I wish
It were a game of Life
Or Monopoly
That I'm playing.
Then if I ran out of money,
Or steam,
I could claim they're cheating,
Get mad and quit,
Or say it's just a game.
But it's not a game,
And I don't know how to quit.
But even if I did
I wonder if I would.
I somehow need the challenge,
Seeing if I can make it
Each time to Go.

Ancient Philosophies that Won't Go Away

Would I be prone to epicureanism or hedonism,
Living for pleasure,
Going out of my way to avoid conflict and pain,
Helping others only if it would benefit me?

Would I be susceptible to stoicism,
Letting "nature" take its course,
Pursuing specific virtues for their own sake,
Believing they will give me a good life?

Could I be a gnostic,
Forgoing established orthodox views,
Devising my own form of knowledge,
Ignoring sin and repentance?

May I never abandon what I know to be true?

Consistency

Will I ever get it right?

Will I try with all my might?

To live the life I should

And not be blinded by my mood?

Can I keep my train of thought

And be humble as I ought,

Ever trusting on the Lord?

In mind of all God's done

Until the crown I've won?

DELAYED PRAISE TO GOD

It's some consolation to know You don't reckon time
The way we do.
I don't always think to thank You for things
Right away.
I sometimes recall something You clearly
Did for me years,
Even decades before,
And wonder if I ever thanked You.
It's embarrassing and humbling to think how
It must have looked to You,
That I appeared so ungrateful,
That I accepted Your healings
And Your mercies as a matter of course,
Without spending time praising You
For Your goodness.

DISCIPLINING BAD BEHAVIOR

It might be well if those of us
Who are disciples of Jesus
Had a blackboard at home.
Then each time we succumb to temptation
We could write 100 times,
"I will disregard the lies of Satan."
We could increase the number
Each time we fail.
The sore hand might in time
Be incentive enough for us to stop
Giving in to the Father of Lies.

GROANINGS OF THE SPIRIT

My mind races with passion, with compassion,
Often following an event where my emotions are stirred,
Seeing people and being led to think of others in my life.
I want to pray, and begin to do so. . .
Things and people dart in and out of my thoughts.
I cannot seem to focus.
I see their needs, their dilemmas, their burdens.
I trust the Lord will take note of the compassion I feel,
That this will be deemed intercession that the Spirit makes,
With groanings that cannot be uttered.

IN APPRECIATION FOR A GREAT LOVE

As I think back on my life
It is clear that one love surpasses all others,
On her part.
I did not earn it or deserve it.
She was somehow compelled to give it,
And more and more, I thank God for it.
When I lived with her,
She prayed for me as I left for work.
She told people how glad she was I was there.
I sense that her prayers for me
Keep me going to this day.
There were times I was too much in my own world
To give her enough notice
When she wanted better companionship.
But she had the capacity to forgive,
And wouldn't want me to dwell on that now.
(Those who claim to have no regrets
When they're near the end,
Well, cannot possibly be telling the truth.)
Yet when I gave her attention

And asked about her life and her family,
It was exhilarating for both of us.
Much did she enjoy talking of her early days,
And I greatly enjoyed hearing of them.
I thank God more and more for the mother I had.

IN THE FROM NOW ON

The from now on can be scary.
What will my health be like?
Will I have dementia?
Will I be able to accomplish what I want,
And have the discipline to do so?
Will I struggle with lethargy?
Will my music stay in me,
Or will it be released to the world?
Will I remember to give glory to God,
The glory He deserves
For what He's done
And what He will do
In the from now on?

JOHN 17

Jesus prayed for me!
John affirms it.
I'm apt to not dwell upon the fact,
To forget it more than I ought.
He prayed not for the world
But to them the Father had given Him,
And to us today who believe on Him
Through the word they preached.
Long before my time
He prayed for me.
How can I not keep that in mind?
I'm grateful for the prayers of others.
May I be aware that Christ heads the list
Of those interceding to the Father
On my behalf,
And live accordingly.

MEMORIES ONLY I CAN VOUCH FOR

We laughed and he smiled when he told us
Jim Croce had a new album out,
Since the singer had been dead for a while.
I'm the only one left to remember that.

I'm grateful for his transportation
To games and concerts
Since I hadn't a car of my own.
I'm the only one left to remember that.

For eighth grade graduation's procession,
Two assigned pairings got switched
At the request of one.
I'm the only one left to remember that.

In grade school I got into a one-sided fight
With someone who didn't seem to like me.
I'm the only one left to remember that.

Once in college I carelessly greeted another
With my own name instead of his,
Simply anticipating the only
Thing he ever seemed to say to me.
I'm the only one left to remember that.

He and I would visit each other in the dorm,
Singing songs we both loved
As we reached the door.
We had similar tastes in music.
I'm the only one left to remember that.

Many such memories I can no longer share
With those involved,
As my contemporaries gradually
Leave for their final destination.

On Suffering a Misreading

"I'm just a soul

Whose intentions are good—

O Lord,

Please don't let me be misunderstood."

Could not have said it better myself.

Face to face, in a letter or email,

Via telephone,

In something I've written—

Grant me one month,

One week, one day—

When my meaning

Isn't taken wrongly.

For one who delights in

Communicating with words

And at times does so successfully,

It is disconcerting,

And bewildering.

I want to blame

The listener or reader,

And ask,
"Where is your brain?
You know that's
Not what I meant.
Did you always score low
On those reading comprehension tests?"
But maybe it's the times we're in.
All want immediate understanding
And not to have to think much
To get the answers they need,
Like a recipe
That uses terms we're familiar with,
Measurements we don't have to convert,
Ingredients we don't have to drive
Into the interior to get,
Or maybe it's me.

PETITION AGAINST ANOTHER VULGAR BIBLE TRANSLATION

Can you imagine Paul ending his letters with "Have a good one"
Or "I'm outta here"?
Or when Jesus asked him on the way to Damascus
why he was persecuting Him,
Paul beginning with, "I mean. . ." or "So. . ."?
Or when Moses protested he was slow of speech,
God telling him, "I know, right?"
Or when anyone offers thanks to God, His response: "No problem"?
Or when Judas realizes his error in betraying the Lord,
exclaiming "My bad"?
Would Luke reminisce of the early days of Peter and Paul saying "Back in the day"?
Would David pause in recounting his experiences of God's mercy
with multiple "I'm like's"?
How about "The Acts of the Disciples" being renamed
"Proactive Disciples"?
How about referring to a conversion experience as a
"Game changer"?

Idioms in earlier ages were, arguably, sweet sounding,
But today's slang, going forward at the end of the day,
is decisively not.

PRAYING BY PERCEPTION

You are my friend,
or family member.
I'm compelled to pray for you.
But it's only natural that my prayer
is based on my perception of you,
of your strengths, your weaknesses,
your faults.
And it's only natural,
if you think to pray for me,
that you do the same,
as shocking as it may be
to learn what you perceive to be my faults,
either shocking that it's true,
or that you know me so little.

REFLECTING ON A GREAT ENIGMA

Billions of people who
Live and have died
Are to be judged
By the righteous Judge.
It's unfathomable,
Incomprehensible,
Past our understanding.
How You'll do it—
How it can be done,
One at a time,
Even assisted by the
Three in One—
How would such a trial
Not take an eternity in itself?
Some things about Your nature, Your ways,
We have but to accept,
And know that You are God,
Yahweh, Jehovah, I Am,
And be ever so mindful
That our lives reflect
Your righteousness.

REFLECTING ON MY FOREBEARS

Though some may think it strange,
I'm compelled to think about my ancestors.
The multitude of family lines each of us has.
The intricate web of overlapping lineages
that only God can grasp.
The physical and character record
that has been passed on to me.
The heritage given me of those who fear God.
I think of those who have dishonored their godly ancestors,
And I like to think that my own would be pleased
that I've given them some thought,
and tried to walk in their ways.
Are they a part of the great cloud of witnesses,
urging us to keep on until we can join them in God's kingdom?
That God arranged all those lines for my background, my story,
and not for me only, but for every one of us,
is something I enjoy to reflect upon,
even while it is utterly beyond my comprehension.

STRIVING FOR PROMOTION

I was given a job in the Trust department.

My three-month review came up.

He told me I'd better keep striving.

I was clearly missing the mark.

He let me down easy,

Mentioned one thing this time.

I must trust Him to keep me consistent.

In another three months

The review came again.

I continued to miss the mark.

An area was added

That I had to correct.

I must trust Him for my health.

My next review

Left me trembling.

Why wasn't I learning my job?

My finances were getting me down.

One thing more that I ought to hand over.

It kept happening with each review.

I was learning about all my failures.

I must trust Him for wisdom,
For relationships,
For soundness of mind.
And especially He reminded,
If I could trust in these things,
The more adept I would be
With sharing His news.
The joy found in that
Would compel me to strive.
I would start to fulfill
The reason I'm here.

The Blessings of the Three

Whether Father, Son or Spirit,
Or the teamwork of the Three,
The blessings they've provided
Have nearly spoiled me.

At night while both watching TV
And editing some prose,
Two thunderclaps did shake the couch
yet produced in me no woes.

Instead I sensed a gentle touch
Of God as though to say:
"I'm with you always; don't forget.
I hear you when you pray."

In a time of heavy rainfall
I prayed I would not crash,
and traffic stopped abruptly,
left me inches from a smash.

I knew God's hand was on me.
I knew He'd heard my cry.
I knew how much He loved me.
I knew He had drawn nigh.

That drive was just the latest
Of many I recall.
He reaches down to uphold me
Or surely I would fall.

He's kept me in employment
And provided for my shelter,
Given me the food I needed,
Maintained my healthy kelter

He's given me abundant friendships,
Folks who've taught me how to live,
How to love and to be thankful,
Even taught me to forgive

God has not withheld his angels,
But dispatches them for me.
They appear before I know it,
Their work a mystery

His blessings are so real,
Yet to tell, ineffable.
I can't fathom why He loves me
All those times I feel unlovable

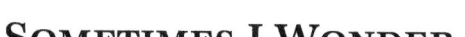

SOMETIMES I WONDER

Why is it that you don't like my honesty?
When I mention my shortcomings
Or my struggles with forgiveness,
You want to suggest counseling.
You think I need therapy.
I think you're just afraid.
You have faults yourselves.
When you hear someone
Admitting his own,
You want to block it out.
The thought of sharing
Your failures with others
Is distasteful.
It would destroy the image
That you have manufactured
For yourselves,
The image that you want
Your obituaries to fully reflect.

THE CHURCH, THE BRIDE

Iron sharpens iron,

It says in Proverbs.

Some can't see,

Or simply ignore,

That we need each other.

They can't find the perfect church,

And stop looking.

They're sure they can make it on their own,

Without fellowship.

Some adhere to the standards

Of their fellow believers

So thoroughly

That they've lost all ability

To think for themselves.

Iron sharpeneth not iron

In such a setting.

Some expect those in a church society

They think they know well

To not deviate from the supposed norm

Of that society,

And when they spot such a deviation,
They feign shock.
L'Engle said the church
Isn't perfect,
Just all we have.
But it's God's Church, His Bride,
And we're called on to honor it,
To stay in it,
And seek ways to improve it.

THE ELUSIVE GENRE

The ideas flow in at such a pace

That I cannot begin to keep up.

But focus on one that I think will work,

And that's when the trouble begins—

Do I have a poem?

Should it be a short story?

How can I get this across?

How 'bout an essay?

That would be grand,

If only I were sure

Of the word count involved.

And then there's the market.

How might this sell?

Do I write what I want,

Let them take it or leave it?

Ah but such a thin line

'tween heart and hack.

What about slant?

Will it be free flowing?

Or aimed at the spiritual,

Modern or commercial?
Yes, I had an idea once,
And before I forget it. . .
I think I'll just tell it to someone.

The Duty Is Mine

Beyond any call of duty

Do you work with me,

Have endless patience with me,

Give me multiple second chances,

Perpetually redeem my much-wasted time.

You make it Your duty

Because of Your love.

It is my duty to demonstrate

My love to You

By doing Your will.

The Jonah Syndrome

Sometimes, no, often, I feel like Jonah.
I know I should talk to someone,
And don't want to do so.
I don't want to forgive someone,
And know I need to.
I know I should make a response,
But I don't feel up to it.
I know I should keep my mouth shut,
But can't bring myself to do so.
I know I should get involved in something,
But am reluctant to do so.
I know I should refrain from involvement,
But find it irresistible.
God forbid He should discontinue
These pleadings of my heart,
Encouraging me to do what I ought,
Rebuking me when I've failed to do so.

THE POWER OF GOD'S WORD

Your Word—

A little goes a long way,

In the best sense.

I wish I knew huge portions.

But when I reflect on what parts I do know,

The results sustain and comfort me.

They give me guidance and assurance.

They bring peace

And grace to help in time of need.

I marvel at the power of Your Word.

The Sin Which Doth So Easily Beset Us

It's true—a cloud of witnesses sees
Things we often can't,
The sin which doth beset us,
That we are blind to,
Though it damage relationships
And nullify our reliability.
We see it in others,
And wonder just what it is
May be seen in us
That we too are unaware of.
These weights can hold us back,
Make us ineffective in our influence,
And all because we don't look unto Jesus
To make our witness sure,
Our reach a wide one,
Our faith complete.

THE SPIRIT BEARING WITNESS AT THE WORKPLACE

I felt the presence of the Holy Spirit when the pre-school girl
Told me to have a nice day.
I sensed His presence when thanked for reaching
For the boy too short to do so.
I felt Him when the Arab man wished me merry Christmas
when I was afraid to do the same for him.
I sense the Holy Spirit beside me when told
That my attitude is pleasant.
I sense Him when handed a tip
For no reason I can discern.
I felt the Holy Spirit prod me
Into righteous indignation when
Returning from break in time to hear
An adherent to a well-known cult
Attempt to proselyte a vulnerable co-worker.
The Third Person gives me assurance
I'm at least partially in the Father's will.

THINGS WE CAN'T KNOW

Who will be at our funerals?
That's one thing we'll never know.
And will they be there for our own sake,
Or the sake of someone we're close to?
Will survivors forge into
A vague plan for a later-date memorial
That today is considered,
And seldom happens?
Perhaps it's out of fear
That no one would come.
Or have we just grown lazy,
Taking 'let the dead bury their dead"
(out of context),
As our justification?
And will the obituaries state the obligatory
"passed away peacefully"?
Will it get to the heart of the lives lived?

THINK IT NOT STRANGE

Think it not strange,

or burdensome,

when God places someone on your mind,

and the impression is so strong

you are compelled to pray for him or her.

You may not especially like the person

or you may have grown fond

and then had to part,

but the compulsion to pray

lingers on, for months, for years.

If the results of your praying

are not seen in this life,

be assured it will be ever so clear to you

in our eternal home with God.

THREATS HIGHLIGHTING GOD'S GOODNESS

If You so much as. . .
Wake me up in the night,
I'll slowly realize You
Desire my fellowship.

If I ever catch You. . .
Blessing me,
I will wonder
Just why You should care.

If that ever happens again. . .
It will likely overwhelm me
And cause me to cry.

If I hear You've. . .
Answered a prayer,
I will marvel at Your kindness.

If Your behavior doesn't change. . .
Me, then I need to have
My heart examined.

TO MY DAD, FIFTY-FIVE YEARS LATER

You called my name in a dream,

Fifty-five years later.

It was great to see you

And hear your voice,

Somehow comforting

To realize that you shaped my life,

Just the same,

Even though I wasn't grown

When you left.

I didn't develop some of your passions.

But I benefited from your good reputation

And the extraordinary family heritage you left.

I learned early to accept myself

And to stand up for who I am

And not let anyone persuade me

To be false to myself.

I've missed your direct influence on my life.

But I can see ways in which

It was yet there all along.

Personalities

And It Is So

Just behind me on a Sunday

Was heard "Amen, amen"—(may it be so).

I shook his hand at the close.

During that week

His physical heart's state

With him did catch up.

The next Sabbath

We're told he's on hospice,

But he was ready to go.

On Monday he began

His real living—Amen—

And it is so!

NEWTON WAS RIGHT

Try as I will
I can never think of a better adjective
for God's grace
than amazing.
Whenever I reflect on how
He has kept me alive and whole
and fitted for Heaven
and out of major trouble
in consequence of my sin
immediately I think of it as,
Amazing,
just as Newton did.

J.T. . . .

. . .they called him,

But to me,

Never comfortable with nicknames,

He was just John.

He died at 45.

At 17, a young girl,

Heavily drunk,

Hit him and his friend

With her vehicle,

Killing the friend

And forever altering John's life.

He was paralyzed,

Never again able to walk,

Vocal cords damaged,

Some brain damage.

I helped take care of him a few years.

I'd often think of him while showering

As he'd scrub his hair vigorously

With his good hand

While proclaiming the virtues of Dove soap.

Whenever he'd forget my name
I'd say it was almost the same
As his middle name, Glennon.
He wasn't dumb,
Knew how to laugh, and tease.
He'd been proud to have been
An altar boy in his church
Before the crash.
I can't imagine being the girl responsible.
I can't imagine being John,
Always wanting to curse her
For what she did,
Always wishing he had been the one to die.
Never being able to fully realize his dreams.
Ever wondering why he had to live with people
With less mental ability than himself,
These thoughts running through his mind
For 28 years.

LeRoy

You may be the first and only person
I never got mad at
until after your death.
You were a friend,
a largely self-educated,
simple yet thinking man
with whom I had things in common.
You read and wrote poetry.
You were a believer in Christ
and His redemption plan.
You had knowledge of your family tree,
and taught me the proper method
for calculating relationships.
Obtaining a certificate
in radio and TV repair,
you made that your life work,
leaving you no retirement plan,
or much accumulation of funds.
When you had to have
daily assistance,
it left you with little to spare each month,
something like forty dollars.

But you didn't complain.
When I went to eat with you,
you insisted on paying for your own.
You left us at age 80
and I went to your estate sale.
Told that there was more upstairs,
I checked it out and was astounded
at the layers of your collected things,
COLLECTIBLES,
things I could have sold for you,
vintage catalogs, magazines, books,
brochures relating to your business.
I grabbed a few things
and sold some for myself.
Why didn't you tell me
you had so much stuff?
No doubt much that was valuable,
and could have gained you some much needed funds.

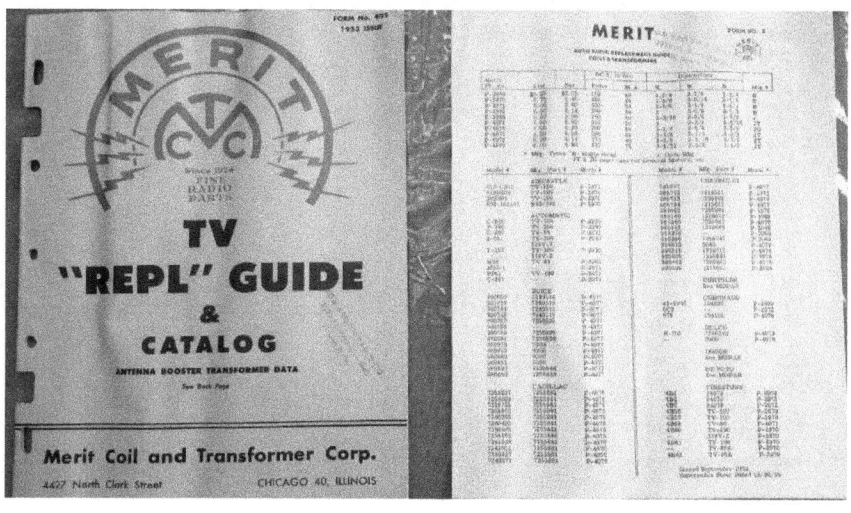

STOPPING PRAYERS FOR A FRIEND

I saw your death notice and I was stunned.
I knew of your longtime health concerns,
and I always prayed for your healing,
and for your salvation.
I've prayed for you for so long
that it will be difficult
to just stop on a dime.
But I'm trusting God
that my prayers have been answered.
He didn't heal you on earth,
but I'm confident that I'll see you again
in His kingdom.

PRAISE

BREVITY OF THE BARRIER

The barrier that creeps
When first I feel the need to pray?
The one the enemy hopes to make
impenetrable?
In no time at all proves
To be but a façade.
With the prayers of others for me,
Both past and present,
God easily breaks through,
Rendering the enemy powerless
To block the passageway
'tween heaven and earth.
For that I am humbled,
Astounded, and ever grateful.

DELIGHTING IN THE LORD

Fun! Of all the words I've thought of
To describe my fellowship with You,
That's the newest one.
It seemed strange at first.
But why should it?
It's a perfect fit
For a friendship that gives me such delight.
The feeling of loneliness
May last for a while.
But in time You turn it around.
And I'm again relishing Your company,
Wondering how I could ever feel
I had no one to commune with,
When You were there all along.

IN REVERENCE OF LANGUAGE

From the Word in the beginning,
To Adam's giving of names,
From Moses and the Law,
To John's writing what he saw,
From the books of the Phoenicians,
Through to Gutenberg's compressions,
You have given us a means
Of making sense of our expressions.
Thank You for the gift of words
That have recorded time and place,
For Your Word and countless lines and hymns
That will lead us to Your face.

JOY UNSPEAKABLE

Thank You, Father,
For being indescribable.
Thank You that words escape us
When we want to express
Our joy thinking of the things
You've done for us.
Language has not been invented
Here on earth
That measures the delights of Heaven,
Or of the heavenly foretaste
We experience here.
So we resort to meditation—
To being still and knowing—
That You are real
And that we'll be better
Equipped to praise You
When we reach Your kingdom.

ON HIS ANSWERING PRAYERS BETIMES

Thank You, Father, for those prayers You answer straightway,
As for health and safety.
Thank You for those that You answer shortly,
as for sustenance.
Those others?
Financial, concerns as to lodging?
You keep me waiting.
But You build my trust.
You shape my character.
You assure me that these things
cannot separate me from Your love.

Psalm 68:19

Blessed be the Lord,
forever and anon
for creating us
for whatever He has for us
past, present, future
who daily loadeth us with benefits,
rest through the night
joy at dawn
food and comfort
assurance of His presence
even the God of our salvation.
offering us eternity with Him
and fellowship in this life
wisdom to endure
peace beyond understanding
Selah.
Pause and consider His works

Rapturous Prayer

When I've broken through to You and

Resisted the enemy in his efforts to keep me from Your presence,

When You've begun to put me in mind of all manner of concerns

For people in my life,

For the triumph of believers around the world,

You give me to understand what needs to happen,

and what I need to talk to You about.

I am then struck with the sense of what a privilege it is to

take my concerns to You.

And I recall that You said we have an Advocate with the Father,

and that You would leave us with the Holy Spirit,

and so many other promises.

And I rejoice that everything You said is true.

Supernal Sounds

I had to turn the music off;
T'was infringing on the wonder
Of the sound of true music aloft,
Gushing rain and booming thunder.
Reminders God is real
And eager to reveal
His presence and His power,
Streaming down from His bower.

THANKING GOD FOR THE UNKNOWN

Although the suspense can be deafening,
at times of uncertainty
You still deserve our praise.
When we don't know what's ahead
and we must trust You,
You are worthy of our thanksgiving.
You force us to transfer
confidence in self
to confidence in our Creator.
To reveal Your plans before their time
would not be in our best interest.
For holding the future in Your hands,
we thank You.
For the trials we undergo,
individually and corporately,
we give You praise.
In that You know the outcome,
we marvel, and we anticipate
things working for our good.

Reprimands

MY PREFERENCES

I prefer a smile to a "how are you?"
I don't know what to say or if you mean it.
I prefer "have a nice day" or "good afternoon" to
"have a good one."
I don't know what that means.
I'd rather hear "you're welcome"
than "no problem."
So often it is said when there
really is a problem.
Don't keep saying
everything is "perfect"
when I'm talking to you.
It shows you're not listening.
Everything can't be perfect.
"Like" can bespeak comparison,
or even affection.
But use it to mean *something*.
"I'm like", "it's like", "he's like", "she's like"
are all meaningless.
I prefer words with meaning.

An Unhealthy Obsession

"What the hell?"
"How in the hell?"
Even "Go to hell."
Most of those "conservative" talk show hosts
don't get it.
Why are they obsessed with hell?
They're conserving the language
They no doubt used in grade school.
Are they even old enough
to have a radio show?
Though many claim adherence
To Christianity or Judaism,
they have no concept
of what hell really is.
If they did, they wouldn't
toss it about so casually.
They fail to realize
what complete separation
from God really entails.
Inhabitants will forever

deeply regret their
rejection of God
while on earth.
Hell's horrors are
indescribable, incomprehensible
and unalterable.
Don't use the term lightly,
unless you intend that
for your destination.

DOCTRINE

Right from the start

It has kept us apart.

It has further divided

Our longtime divisions.

It has left undecided

Many a skeptic who

Deem the gospel untrue

Since we all struggle to agree.

Such diverse points of view

Cause their share of derisions

From those who need for to see

That their purpose they can renew.

Identify not with your church's canon,

Which alas will be gone anon.

Identify best with your Savior,

Who undeniably you has favored.

Recall 17th of John,

The true Lord's Prayer,

When He prayed we all would be one,

Just as the Father and Son.

Take up my dare

To use only essentials,
Not doctrinal credentials,
To show unbelievers we care.

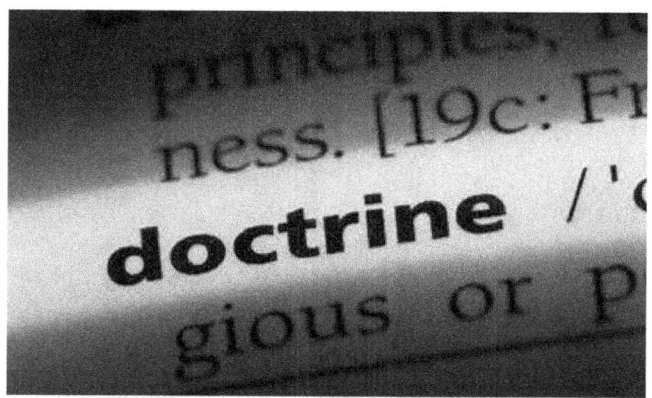

On Asking "How Are You?"

When you ask me "how are you?"
And you're practically a stranger,
It puts me in a bind.
Do I mutter something
About my state of affairs,
Risking total silence
And unconcern
On your part?
Or do I let it ride,
Never knowing
If the question was sincere?
I'd rather not talk of my troubles
To someone who only asks
Because he can't think of
Anything else to say.

QUESTIONABLE REQUEST

"Pray for me as I try to sing."

We've heard it a lot in the church.

What does that mean?

I really don't know.

It seems a rather last-minute request.

If you feel unprepared or ill,

Why are you trying to sing?

Shouldn't we be praying

That the words of the song

Be understood and taken to heart?

That they complement the coming sermon?

Shouldn't the focus be on the song

And its meaning for the worshiper,

And not really on the singer?

SPIRITUAL TRUTHS

An Enduring Legacy

Many perchance envy him,
The thief upon the cross,
The one who asked the Lord to remember him.
His salvation was assured by the Savior Himself,
And just at the point of death.
He didn't have to go through years
Of struggle to live the Christian life,
While you and I are compelled to set an example,
To proclaim the news that's good.
But he did give proof
Of the very immediacy and simplicity
Of the gospel message.
His one act of repentance gave assurance
To countless souls throughout the ages,
Assurance that a simple act of faith
Could set them free.

A Perplexing, Disturbing Reality of Today

While the earth remains,
Promised the Father,
Seedtime and harvest,
Cold and heat,
Summer and winter,
Day and night
Shall not cease.
Why do the doomsayers
Ignore this, and not believe God?
It is written in the Psalms,
The Lord is clothed with strength;
The world also is stablished,
He has laid the foundations of the earth,
That it should not be removed forever.
It cannot be moved,
Or shaken, in a global sense,
Though localized earthquakes
And calamities will occur.
Why do the nations spend money
And alter our lifestyles,

Contradicting God's Word,
Believing they can improve
On what God has declared
Unalterable?

BEYOND THE CROSS

The week before perhaps is when it started,
the anguish, the doubts, the loneliness.
You felt You couldn't reach the Father,
that he was silent and gave no answer.
That in itself was a glimpse of hell.
Your friends forsook You,
preferring to sleep, denying, betraying You.
You asked the Father to ease the pain,
yet You knew that this was His plan.
You had to be the sacrifice.
and like Abel's, it was pleasing to God.
Thank You for enduring that week on our account.

ENOUGH

Al-
though it
seems the earth
will go on and
on the time will come
when God will have enough
of people replacing Him with
things or even themselves and call
for an end to this age and proceed
with plans to build a new heaven and earth.

Fulfilment

In the fullness of time
You shined Your light on the world,
Your appearance foretold by God's prophets.
It's what we believe and know to be true.
Your life alone was a life
Long predicted, along with
Your passion and suffering,
Your plan for salvation,
Your kingdom on earth
That prepares for us a place in Your heaven.
How can the world not believe such a truth,
When all things that were told of You
Have since come to pass,
All but Your return to earth,
Your coming through the line
Of Jesse and David,
Your conception by God's Holy Spirit,
Empowering the young girl Mary,
Your authority over the earth
That is greater than that of the enemy?
You have set us apart

Since we called on Your name,
But command us to spread
The good news of Your love.

FORGOTTEN PAST

You don't know my past—
What a thought*!
You know my parentage
And my heritage,
My schooling and career,
My insecurities,
Weaknesses and strengths.
But forgiven sins?
They're forgotten by the Father,
Son and Spirit.
They're seldom thought of.
When they are it's the Enemy
Trying to discourage me
And cause me to feel
Nothing's changed,
One of the many lies of satan
I must refute each day.

HIS PROMISES, MY TASKS

Father, I claim them all:
The perfect peace that passes understanding,
The direction of my paths,
The mercy and grace to help me
In my time of need,
The working of all things together for my good,
My every need supplied,
Your strength enabling me to do all things.
May I do my part:
Keeping my mind on You,
Letting my requests be made known to You,
Trusting in You with all my heart,
Never trusting my own understanding,
Coming boldly unto Your throne.

NUMERICAL REMINDERS

A digital clock conveys Scriptural references,

A thing seen every day

That gives me reminders

Of the truths in God's word.

Or it brings to mind a birthday

Of someone I need to pray for.

Seeing 316 reminds me of

God's love that compelled Him

To send His Son to die for me.

320 tells me that Jesus will fellowship with me

Each time I invite Him.

139 reminds that I can never

Count God's thoughts toward me,

And that He knew me before I was fully formed.

53 recalls how Christ's sufferings

For me were predicted centuries before they happened.

I am assured that God leads me as a shepherd

And never leaves me when I see 23.

That Christ alone can bring about our salvation

Is reinforced by 412.

13 reminds me of what true love is.

Proof that Jesus prayed for me
long before my lifetime
Amazes me again with 17.

Psalm 19

The moderns fail to realize

That God's Word and His laws

Will clear things up for them

If they'll only give heed.

David explains—His laws are perfect,

Just what we need to turn from wrong thinking.

They are sure, giving wisdom without respect of person.

They are right, giving us gladness of heart.

His statues are pure, enabling us to see things better.

They are clean and will last forever

True and righteous altogether are God's commands.

ROMANS 5

I have often found it strange
that the older I get
the more my hope increases.
But knowing Paul's progression
brings understanding.
My hope is preceded by experience
in living the Christian life,
in seeing how God has met my needs.
Before this was patience
that we all need to develop
to get through the tribulation
that we were never promised
we'd be free from.

THE ONE WITH BREATH, WIND AND FIRE

To think of the Persons of the Trinity—
It's humbling for us—
and makes us feel so small.
We cannot fathom the omnipresence of the One
sent to earth, the Holy Spirit,
how He goes about guiding, interceding,
teaching, convincing us of sin,
speaking through the Scriptures,
how He does these things for all believers,
all at once.
To think on this thrills us
and gives us a desire
to feel more of His presence.
As we think more on Him
the cares of our lives become smaller
and more manageable.
We are grateful for the knowledge
we have here on earth,
and can hardly wait for the time
when that knowledge will be complete.

YE ARE THE SALT OF THE EARTH

Ye are the salt of the earth,
admonished the Lord to His own.
Ye are the light of the world,
He further set the tone.
From the time of your new birth,
the world should know your worth,
and that you are reliable
and of good repute.
But the world fails to see
your power to preserve and
To keep it from destruction.
The world doesn't know
that the salt of the earth
is the cause of their holding on
and being kept afloat.
The more you're willing to serve
God and others in honesty
the better chance folks have
of being made free.

SUPPLICATION

A Prayer for More Steadfastness

My memory is much too short.
You grant me glorious times
of intense awareness of Your presence,
at times in the night,
and sometimes after dawn,
times when You lead me through
what and whom I need to pray for,
times when I have a supernatural
sense of the Spiritual world,
times when You assure me
that the power I have in You
is greater than that the enemy
affords to those around me
who do not serve You.
But how swiftly I forget
Your graciousness in giving
me those extraordinary times.
And it takes me some time
to get back to where we were,
You and I, with that extreme closeness.
Forgive me for not pursuing those times
on a more regular basis.

A Prayer for Writers

The written word has power to change,

To change the mind of the one who reads.

Words can set a pattern for a way of seeing things.

May my words be ever honest, ever piercing, ever bold.

May they never once mislead nor be confusing,

And never give the wrong instructions.

It is only in eternity that I'll ever know their impact.

Until then I need to pray that my words bring change for good.

A Prayer to Be Used of God

Though my faults are all
too obvious to me,
when lingers my
sense of inadequacy,
You give me work to do.
That makes me akin to Moses,
to Jacob, to David, to Peter,
and others.
Your strength is made perfect
in my weakness.
May my steadfast goal through
life be to overcome
the enemy and his lies,
his efforts to see to my defeat,
and continue to be of use
in the expansion of Your Kingdom
until such time as I abide there with You.

ADJUST MY SENSES

Lord, clear my ears when You speak.
Clog them when it's the enemy.
Sharpen my eyesight to see your workings.
Blind me to faults in others.
May I feel compassion for those with needs,
and feel nothing when I'm wronged.
Let me taste Your goodness, Your mercy,
and have no taste for what's wrong.

ATTRIBUTES OF GOD REQUIRING ACTION FROM ME

Your thoughts toward me
number more than grains of sand.
Increase my thoughts
toward You.
You knew me before I was
formed in the womb.
Increase my knowledge of You.
Nothing can separate me
from Your love.
May I strive to be worthy of that love.
Your mercies toward me
are new every morning.
May I begin each day
focused on You.
You've prepared for me things
I cannot comprehend.
May I keep that in mind
day by day.

FOR THE PEOPLE I HAVE KNOWN

Names and faces

from childhood and through the years,

in sundry places,

my elders and my peers—

bring them to mind

in the night and through the day.

For them let me find,

let me take the time to pray.

Acknowledging those,

both known and unaware,

who bring my foes and woes

before You in earnest prayer.

Psalm 34

May I not let the Enemy keep me from knowing
That the answer's right there in Your Word,
That before all my fears, all my doubts can start showing,
I'll have heeded those things I have heard,
How that David was heard when he sought for the Lord
And delivered from all that he feared.
He learned and he taught that the one healthy fear
Is the fear of the only true God.

Reality

I've heard it said,
And I believe it—
The spiritual world is more real
Than the physical world.
Its reality is greater
Because it's eternal,
And what's physical now
On earth is only temporal.
When I'm aware of the Holy Spirit,
And His presence,
Things go well with me.
When I can sense the angels around me,
I know I have protection.
When I realize that satan
Is the father of lies,
I learn to not believe his lies.
Awaken the spiritual realm in me, Lord.
Keep me in tune with what is real.

REPROVING RESTLESSNESS

When I sense I've spoken wrong,
Keep me restless.
When my prayer has been neglected,
Keep me restless.
When I've not stayed in Your Word,
Keep me restless.
When my doubts exceed my trust,
Keep me restless
When my anger's misdirected,
Keep me restless.
When I don't speak up for truth,
Keep me restless.
May my restlessness prevail
'til I repent.

SINCERITY IN PRAYER

That God hears my petitions
I have reason to believe.
I tell Him my ambitions,
How that He would give me leave
To do greater things for Him,
Overcoming Satan's scoff.
To retain the things I've asked Him
Is where confidence leaves off—
That those things once said in prayer
Be true longings of my heart.

Toward an Eternal Curriculum Vitae

Lord, grant that the *summary* of my life win Your approval;

When I have fallen, let me *resume* my walk with You.

May my *objective* be to fully know You;

If I be worthy, provide me with a *membership* to Your kingdom.

May I have no *hobby* contrary to Your principles;

May I receive no *education* You would not consent to.

Let all my *experiences* serve to increase my trust in You;

May I always *honor* those who have pointed me to You.

And, Jesus, if I've done all this, *refer* me to Your Father;

May I count no *award* greater than to hear Him say, "Well done."

FIRST NAME **LAST NAME**

Address · Phone
Email · LinkedIn Profile · Twitter/Blog/Portfolio

To replace this text with your own, just click it and start typing. Briefly state your career objective, or summarize what makes you stand out. Use language from the job description as keywords.

EXPERIENCE

DATES FROM – TO
JOB TITLE, COMPANY
Describe your responsibilities and achievements in terms of impact and results. Use examples, but keep it short.

DATES FROM – TO
JOB TITLE, COMPANY
Describe your responsibilities and achievements in terms of impact and results. Use examples, but keep it short.

EDUCATION

MONTH YEAR
DEGREE TITLE, SCHOOL
It's okay to brag about your GPA, awards, and honors. Feel free to summarize your coursework too.

MONTH YEAR
DEGREE TITLE, SCHOOL
It's okay to brag about your GPA, awards, and honors. Feel free to summarize your coursework too.

SKILLS

- List your strengths relevant for the role you're applying for
- List one of your strengths
- List one of your strengths
- List one of your strengths
- List one of your strengths

ACTIVITIES

Use this section to highlight your relevant passions, activities, and how you like to give back. It's good to include Leadership and volunteer experiences here. Or show off important extras like publications, certifications, languages and more.

THE WEAK WORKER

Ambassador-at-large should be my role
With headquarters moving through my day,
Reflecting best my Savior is my goal
Though at times I fail Him miserably.
Why I'm kept on the payroll, I don't know.
I learn but slight, am quick with slip of tongue
And sometimes feel my progress is but slow.
His patience is incomprehensible.
His continual love an unfathomable wonder.
How can His thoughts toward me be so high,
When at times my life seems one great blunder?
Lord, use me to expand Your kingdom.
Use me in spite of myself and my failure,
To help prepare more people for heaven,
To see crowds of people most peculiar.

WORD STUDIES

ABIDE: A WORD STUDY

My desire is to abide,

To wait until endued with power from on high,

To stand firm when tempted,

To remain prayerful until I receive an answer,

To encounter trials courageously,

And not accept defeat,

To remain steadfast until the work is done,

To await clear instructions before proceeding,

To submit to the will of God,

To tolerate persecution when for a righteous cause.

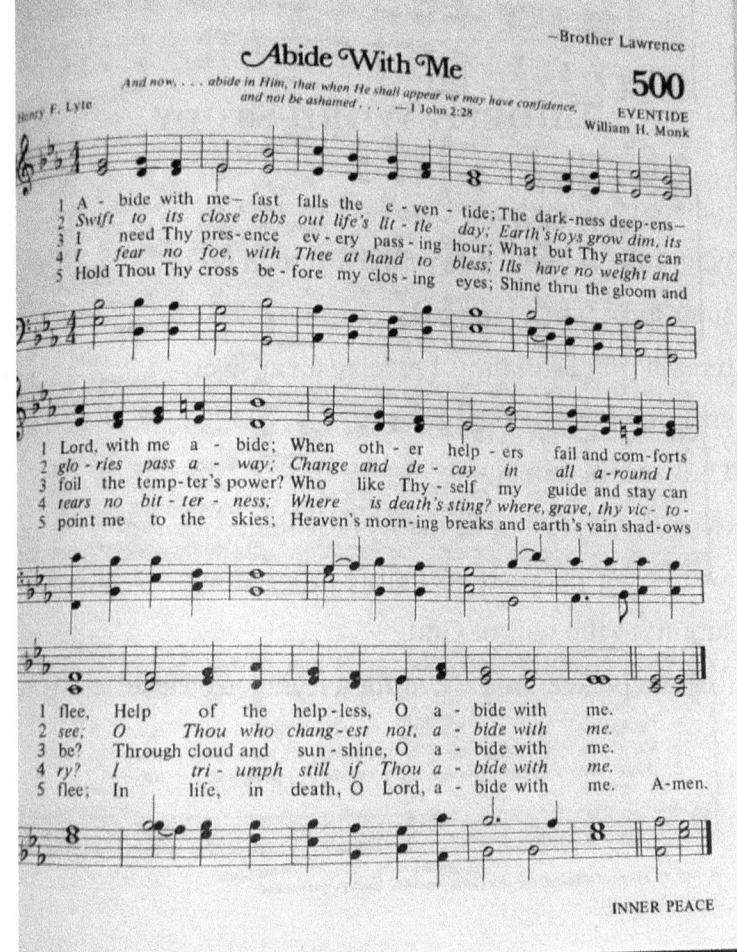

Fear: A Word Study

I desire a healthy Fear,
One that mingles dread
And reverence toward God,
One that makes me anxious
For the salvation of friends and family.
Give me no doubt
That God is able to inspire
The fear of Himself
Into those He puts on my heart.
Give me the understanding
That God's holiness requires
Steps taken by each of us
To ascertain a right
Relationship with Him.

No Further Translating Needed

Beautiful words!
Wondrous concepts!
Because of God's loving-kindness,
He is long-suffering.
Being long-suffering,
He extends His loving-kindness
Not willing that any perish,
He waits and waits,
and waits still more
The God of multiple second chances
for both the believer and the lost.
Long-suffering, He's uncannily patient.
His tenderness and compassion
reflect His loving-kindness.
No other English words are needed
to express these attributes of God.
They conjure a picture that
can hardly be applied to humans.
Thank you, Coverdale and Tyndale,
for compounding these words,
to give us an accurate concept of the Father.

TRESPASS: A WORD STUDY

Forgive us our trespasses, Lord,
for trespasses left open
lead to death.
They *offend* you,
and *violate* the conditions
of the law required by Your holiness.
When we judge another's actions
unmercifully we *intrude* into territory
reserved for Your righteous judgment.
For our *sins* we deserve to *die,*
a lasting, spiritual death,
much worse than any physical.

TRESPASS

1428 *Surtees Misc.* (1888) 5 His trespas
utteryng of fals osmunds and castyng of
Rolls of Parlt. VI. 157/1 Trespasses doo
armes ayenst your peas. **1553** T. W
Sometimes a man is accused of felonye, ar
his offence to be but a trespace. **1651** G. W
211 The word Trespasse..comprehends
the Law. But our discreet Lawyers call or
Trespasses, and make distinctions even arr
POLLOCK & MAITLAND *Hist. Eng. Law* II
Trespass (*transgressio*) is the most general
it will cover all or almost all wrongful :
Every felony, says Bracton, is a trespa
trespass is not a felony. In a narrowe
trespass is used [in 13th c.] as a contrast t

β. *c* **1308** in *Pol. Songs* (Camden) 197 Of
hede, Al thilk trepas is a-go.

3. *Law. spec.* Any actic
committed against the person c
another; also short for *action of t*

a. *trespass to person.*

13.. *Cursor M.* 29391 (Cott. Galba)
light trispase To prest or clerk vnwitand

About the Author

A lifelong Missourian, Glen Lowell Blesi was born in Sullivan in Franklin County. He has long had an interest in local history and family history. He began efforts to write for publication some 40 years ago and has written numerous articles in those areas, as well as inspirational. Other writing interests are poetry and book reviews. The seventh of eight siblings, he presently lives in southwestern Missouri near his son, daughter and son-in-law.

Previously Published works by Blesi

"Toward an Eternal Curriculum Vitae" first appeared in the October 18, 1992 issue of *Standard*.

"In Reverence of Language" first appeared in the Summer 2003 issue of *The Discerning Poet*.

"The Weak Worker" first appeared in the March / April 2022 issue of *Bible Advocate*.

"His Promises, My Tasks" first appeared in the September / October 2023 issue of *Bible Advocate*.

www.ingramcontent.com/pod-product-compliance
Lightning Source LLC
Chambersburg PA
CBHW072021060426
42449CB00033B/1463